"Nobody knows the mind and heart of the catechist better than Gwen Costello! No sooner does the *General Directory for Catechesis* call for more attention to the spirituality of the catechist, than Gwen Costello provides us with *A Prayerbook for Catechists*; a true blessing of a book. The prayers that Gwen provides in these pages come from her own experience as a religious educator and will touch the soul and lift the spirit of any catechist!"

Joe Paprocki,
Author, *Tools for Teaching*

"The best thing DREs can give their catechists is this book. Feeling connected and supported is imperative for effective teaching, and this is the feeling that permeates this book. Gwen shares prayers about concerns so familiar teachers will think she's read their minds! Spanning the school year, 'from the first day to the last,' these short, simple, honest prayers reflect hopes and frustrations, triumphs and failures recognizable to all catechists. Best of all, Gwen models a direct, intimate style that will encourage catechists to 'open up' and share their own special needs with Jesus, the master teacher.

Carole MacClennan, Author

"Another right-on-target book from the pen of a talented author! As I read through the prayers, I could envision each situation...and each prayer touched a responsive chord in my own mind and heart. Any catechist who prays them will find in them a source of comfort, guidance, and insight for their ministry."

Alison Berger, Editor and Author

"The prayers in this book are a reminder of the importance of praying for the students in our class and asking for God's help in all that we do. They speak to both new and experienced catechists who are sharing their faith journey with God's children. This would be a wonderful gift book because it speaks to the heart and experiences of catechists everywhere."

Patricia Mathson,
Author, *70 Sacrament Starters for Children*

"Here are prayers for times of doubt, apprehension, panic, hope, and excitement. They reassure catechists that these feelings are common and also offer assurances on a grander scale that God is with them as they teach. The mantra-like phrase at the end of each prayer help catechists go through a day like Tevye in *Fiddler on the Roof*: praying simply and casually and drawing comfort from our 'every day' God."

Anne E. Neuberger,
Columnist, *Religion Teacher's Journal*,
Author, *A Circle of Saints*

A Prayerbook for Catechists

GWEN COSTELLO

TWENTY THIRD 23rd
PUBLICATIONS
www.23rdpublications.com

For all the catechists in my own life
who have shared with me
in the great ministry
of proclaiming the presence
of the Risen Christ.

1st printing of revised edition 2009

TWENTY-THIRD PUBLICATIONS
A Division of Bayard
One Montauk Avenue, Suite 200
New London, CT 06320
(860) 437-3012
(800) 321-0411

ISBN 978-0-89622-979-2
Printed in the U.S.A.

CONTENTS

INTRODUCTION

One year the children in my religion class were hyperactive—and that's putting it mildly. I thought that was the worst scenario for a catechist. The next year, however, the group was so passive that I could never tell what the children were thinking or feeling—ever. With hindsight that active bunch looked pretty good!

Kids come in all guises and sizes, but whether too active or too quiet, or even just perfect, all of us catechists share similar joys, concerns, and feelings about those we teach. We are sometimes apprehensive, sometimes enthusiastic, discouraged, appalled, delighted, surprised, despondent, elated, tired, energetic—and you can add to this list yourself, no doubt.

The prayers here try to put into words some of these feelings and concerns. They are based on my own experiences, of course, but also on the experiences of many other catechists who have shared their stories with me over the years.

Though these prayers span a typical teaching year, you can, of course, pray them anytime you want. So, choose the prayers you like best and stay with them as long as you like.

You'll notice that at the bottom of each prayer there is a one-liner that sums it up. These mantra-like phrases are easy to remember and are meant to be repeated often throughout any given day. Also scattered throughout the book are reflective statements from the *General Directory for Catechesis* (as they appear in *The General Directory for Catechesis in Plain English* from Twenty-Third Publications). These are meant to motivate and inspire you to imitate the teaching methods and attitudes of Jesus.

The goal of any book of prayers, this one included, is to inspire you to pray in your own words, to take your concerns to God daily, even hourly, knowing that God hears and answers you and loves and cares about you deeply.

Jesus Christ is the first catechist. He was not only teacher but also friend to his disciples. He lived what he preached. He asked opportune questions and he introduced them to prayer.

General Directory for Catechesis in Plain English, #137

A NEW BEGINNING

Dear God,
You know how nervous I am!
My mind says,
"Don't be ridiculous;
    they're just kids."
But my emotions say otherwise.
What if I start out all wrong,
get off on the wrong foot?
What if the children are hard to
    control?
What if they simply won't listen?
What if they don't like me?
What if, what if....

Be with me loving God,
to strengthen me and guide me.
Keep your hand on me
as I begin anew
to proclaim your holy Word,
to share my Catholic faith.

Holy Spirit, my helper, inspire me.
Jesus, my Savior, shine
    through me. Amen.

To truly help a person encounter God, which is the task of the catechist, means to emphasize the relationship that the person has with God so that he or she can be guided by God.

General Directory
for Catechesis in
Plain English, #139

Keep your hand on me, dear God.

YOU KNOW THEIR NAMES

Great and loving God,
I do believe that every child
I will be teaching is unique
and that you know each by name.
Each has a distinct personality,
and special gifts and qualities—
as well as flaws and weaknesses!

I want to think of these children
not only as a class, but as individuals
that I will come to love and respect.
Teach me to be patient
with the ones who will often
    interrupt
and with the ones who will never
    sit still.
Help me to understand
that one plan does not fit all.

I really don't know how
I will meet each child's learning
    needs, dear God,
But they are your children,
    and I will rely on you.
Help me to teach as you
    want me to. Amen.

*The ministry
of catechists
is inspired by
faith itself and
by Christ's own
teaching style.
Under the
guidance of the
Spirit it leads
people to a true
experience of faith.*

General Directory
for Catechesis in
Plain English, #143

May I
love your
children,
great God.

I HOLD THEM OUT TO YOU

Here in my hands, Jesus, great teacher,
are the names of the children
    in my class.
Sixteen names representing sixteen
unique and gifted children.
I do believe that each is blessed by you
with special qualities and talents,
with an individual personality
and a particular ability to learn.

I hold each of these children out
    to you
and ask your special blessing
    on them.
Open their minds and hearts
that they might hear your message
in spite of the limitations
    of my lessons.
Speak to them through me
and teach them through me
that you are with them always,
loving and forgiving,
challenging and rewarding.
Shine through me, Jesus,
that each of these sixteen children
may know and understand
your mysterious presence in
    their lives. Amen.

God's wonderful dialogue with every human being is the inspiration for catechesis. Hence it is neither of a purely divine form, without human interests, nor merely of human form without the divine presence.

General Directory
for Catechesis in
Plain English, #144

Shine
through
me, great
teacher
Jesus.

5

I REALLY LOST IT

Loving and forgiving God,
I made a mistake today.
It was only my second class,
    and I lost my temper.
After telling the children
    at least five times
to settle down and be quiet,
I really lost it.
I yelled, I threatened, and
    then I just sat down.
The children were shocked into silence.

I was immediately sorry
for giving such bad example,
but I couldn't say a word.
One of the children said, "We're sorry,"
and I looked up and saw
that they were more afraid
    of me than sorry.
Then I said, "I'm sorry too,"
    and I meant it.
I went on with the lesson,
but it just wasn't the same.

Forgive me, loving God, for not knowing
how to handle such situations.
Forgive me for that moment of weakness.
Help me to do better next time. Amen.

*Genuine catechesis
helps discern the
action of God
in the life of the
believer through a
climate of listen-
ing, thanksgiving,
and prayer.*

General Directory
for Catechesis in
Plain English, #145

Pardon me
when I fail,
forgiving
God.

EACH CHILD IS UNIQUE

I know in theory, Jesus my Savior,
that each child has to learn about you
and the things of God, at
    his or her own pace
and with unique learning abilities.

And yet, in practice, I demand
    the same of all.
I expect all to be attentive when I speak,
interested in my questions,
enlightened by my insights—
and it isn't working.
Help me, Jesus, to be flexible,
to allow for a variety of learning styles
in every lesson I prepare.
I know it can be done,
because other catechists
    and teachers do it.

I know that I will have to devote
more time and thought
to understanding each child's
    way of learning.
And I will need your help,
    because without you,
I will try to make one lesson fit all.
Guide me, shove me, strengthen me
to do this and to do it well. Amen.

God speaks to us in ways we can understand. Likewise catechesis must seek a language that effectively communicates the word of God. Only by God's grace can this be done. The Holy Spirit gives us the joy of doing it.

General Directory
for Catechesis in
Plain English, #146

———————

Help me,
Jesus, to be
open and
flexible.

7

I'M ACTUALLY EXCITED

Here I am, God of all goodness,
standing before you
surprisingly full of energy
    and enthusiasm.
I'm actually excited about
    my teaching.
In just a few classes I have come
    to know
the children by name and a little about
their personalities and learning styles.
A few of them even seem glad
to be in my religion class!

Be with me today
as I spend time with them,
pray with them,
search with them,
and celebrate your presence
    with them.

Holy and great God,
I praise you for giving
these children of yours
into my care.
Speak through me, please.
Amen.

The catechist must know and use those educational tools and methods that can be applied in this ministry. There is a connection between method and content, with method at the service of content.

General Directory
for Catechesis in
Plain English, #147-149

I praise you,
God of all
goodness.

TEACHING ABOUT VIRTUE

Jesus, my Savior and friend,
my lesson today
is about living a Christian life.
I'm supposed to talk about virtues
and the gifts of the Holy Spirit.
But how can I teach about things
I find so difficult to practice myself?
What can I say about love,
patience, kindness,
wisdom, and compassion,
when I myself am sometimes
unkind, impatient,
foolish, and judgmental?

Help me, please, to rely on you,
to let you speak through me.
May your children see and hear,
not just me, but you.
May they experience
your presence
in all that I say and do.
Amen.

We must always remember that the communication of faith is an event of grace. Simply put, God is acting in people's lives.

General Directory
for Catechesis in
Plain English, #150

Be with me,
Jesus, in all
I say and do.

MAY I BE HUMBLE

Come Holy Spirit,
Great teacher and guide,
    I need your help.
My lesson this week is about forgiveness,
and my manual says to assign roles
so the children can act out
the story of the prodigal son.
The last time I tried role-playing,
the class got totally out of hand.
It took me ten minutes to
    calm everyone down.

What did I do wrong?
Other catechists seem to
    do such activities
with no problem at all.
Am I that inexperienced?
Is there some magic formula
no one told me about?
If I hadn't been so embarrassed
about the noise and the commotion,
I would have asked my DRE for help.
Maybe I just have to postpone
any more role-playing
until I DO get help.
May I be humble enough to ask. Amen.

Catechesis has the task of making people more aware of their most basic human experiences so they become aware of God's hand in their lives.

General Directory for Catechesis in Plain English, #153

Keep me humble, great teacher and guide.

A "FRIENDLY" VISIT

O God, giver of all good gifts,
today I need the gift of humility.
My DRE will be sitting in
    on my class—
just a friendly visit,
but what if I don't do very well?
My lesson is planned,
but what if the children
    don't respond?
Will she think I didn't prepare?
Here I go again...
What if, what if, what if?

Help me to rely on you,
and should my class not go well,
help me to accept that fact,
knowing that I did the best I could.

O God, giver of all good gifts,
give the children I teach
the gift of good behavior,
today in particular.
Amen.

*Human experience
points to the divine
because there is
an inborn hunger
for union with
God. Reflection
on experience is
therefore necessary
if the truths of
Revelation are
to be understood
at all.*

General Directory
for Catechesis in
Plain English, #153

———————

I need
the gift of
humility,
O God.

A DISRUPTIVE CHILD

Holy Spirit,
Spirit of the risen Christ,
I need your help in a
    particular way today.
One of the kids in my class
is so out of control
that I can't finish a sentence
without being interrupted.
She goes non-stop and I can't keep up.
Worst of all, she is distracting
    the other children
and we're all going nowhere fast.

After two months of this, I
    have had enough.
Give me courage, please,
to be honest with my DRE,
to admit that this child is
    too much for me.

Holy Spirit, bless this child too
and help her to know that
    I care about her;
I just can't handle this situation.

Walk with me today.
Amen.

Experience is, in fact, the very place in human life where salvation occurs. The catechist must teach the person to read his or her own lived experience so as to see in it God reaching us with grace and saving us.

General Directory
for Catechesis in
Plain English, #153

Give me
courage,
Spirit of the
risen Christ.

TAKING THE EASY WAY

Holy Spirit, all knowing, all loving God,
you know and love the
    children in my class.
You know how each one learns
and what each needs most from me.

Oh, I do get it right from time to time,
but only when I remember that
    each child is unique
and deserves to be taught as such.
I too often fall back on methods
that are the easiest for me,
reading the text, asking questions,
and talking on and on.
I know in my heart
that only the most attentive children
can effectively learn this way.
I forget about the timid ones,
    the active ones,
the ones who need to see,
    hear, touch, and say.
They require so much more
than I'm sometimes willing to give.
Give me a boost, Holy Spirit,
and inspire me to teach every child
in precisely the way each needs
    to be taught. Amen.

*It is important
that the disciple be
formed in the faith,
and not merely
taught facts about
faith, even though
the facts of the faith
are important in
the journey toward
mature faith.*

General Directory
for Catechesis in
Plain English, #155

Give me
a boost,
loving
Holy Spirit.

ANGELS AND SAINTS

All you angels and saints of God,
pray for me please as I prepare
    with my class
to celebrate the feast of All Saints.
I love this feast
because it says that all of us,
every single one of us,
is called by God,
as all of you were,
to give thanks and praise.

Teach us, guide us, show us how
to share the joy of our calling,
to reach out to one another,
to listen, to share, to comfort,
to console one another,
to encourage one another when we fail,
to pray for one another when we falter.

It's a great feast, and I want the children
to know what a privilege it is
to be among the communion of saints.

I know, of course,
that they are more concerned
    about Halloween
because of its fun and festivity,
costumes and candy.
It's a hard act to follow.

But help me to make a dent,
dear friends of God.
Help those I teach
to look to you for guidance,
to learn from you,
how to be children of God
and followers of Jesus Christ.
Amen.

*Nothing—not
the method or
the texts, or any
other part of the
program—is more
important than
the person of the
catechist.*

General Directory
for Catechesis in
Plain English, #156

Inspire me, please,
all you angels and saints.

IN THANKSGIVING

Gracious God, giver of all good things,
as Thanksgiving approaches,
I want to pause and say thanks
for all your gifts and graces,
especially the ones I have received
as your catechist.

Thank you for the gift of faith,
which is so life-giving and so much more
than doctrines or definitions can convey.
Thank you for the gift of hope,
which is so full of promise
and fills me with such longing
to know you more fully.
Thank you for the gift of love,
that can never be contained or explained
by our creeds and commandments.

Thank you for each child in my class,
each so unique, so mysterious,
    so challenging.
Thank you above all for my call
to proclaim the way of Jesus.
Amen.

The gifts given to the catechist by the Spirit to witness faithfully and live accordingly are the very soul of catechetical ministry.

General Directory for Catechesis in Plain English, #156

Thank you, God, giver of all good things.

Jesus, beloved Savior,
it's getting closer to Advent,
a season I feel very strongly about.
I want my class to know
that waiting for your birth
is a spiritual experience,
a time of waiting different
from all other waiting.
I see their eyes light up
when I say the word "Christmas,"
but not for the reasons I would like.

How can I make a difference
in the little time I have with them?
How can I observe Advent
	with these children
in a meaningful way, in a way that will
touch their hearts and change
	their lives?
I know for certain that I can't do a
	thing
without your help.
Let your Advent light shine
	through me.
Amen.

*The catechist
is a mediator,
facilitating
communication
between people and
the mystery of God.*

General Directory
for Catechesis in
Plain English, #156

Jesus,
beloved
Savior, help
me touch
their hearts.

TO BE LIKE MARY

Mary, mother of Jesus, and my mother,
as Christmas draws near,
my thoughts turn to you.
There must have been times
when you had a roomful of kids,
lively children full of energy
and hungry (perhaps
    without knowing it)
for the Spirit of the living God.

What did you do?
How did you quiet them
and talk to them
about God's place in their lives?

As I begin to plan for my
last class before Christmas,
I ask you to pray for me
that I might radiate God's presence
as you must have done.
I want God's light to shine through me
that I might draw those I teach to Jesus,
the light of the world, the
    prince of peace,
our blessed Savior, your
    beloved son. Amen.

The catechist is called to a Christian way of life that reflects his or her beliefs. The relationship between the catechist and those to be catechized is also very important.

General Directory
for Catechesis in
Plain English, #156

Mary,
my mother,
pray for me.

A NEW YEAR BEGINS

Blessed Savior, source of all life,
we are beginning a new calendar year,
and it offers me a chance
to begin anew with those I teach.
My new year's resolution is
to be a more enthusiastic catechist.

But how can I carry through?
What can I possibly do or say
to make the time worthwhile
for the children you have
    placed in my care?
Warm me up, please,
with the fire of your presence.
Touch my reluctant heart and
    be with me as I try
to touch the hearts of your "little ones"
with my own joy and enthusiasm.

With you, dear Savior, I
    can do all things.
Without you I can do nothing.
Come along with me to every class
and be our "unseen guest,"
the one who lights the way for
    the children and me
with great joy and enthusiasm. Amen.

Those to be catechized cannot be passive recipients but must be actively engaged in the process through prayer, participation in the sacraments, the liturgy, parish life, social commitments, works of charity, and the promotion of human values.

General Directory
for Catechesis in
Plain English, #157

———————

Blessed
Savior, be
our "unseen
guest."

I'LL KEEP ON TRYING!

Holy Spirit, my comforter and guide,
it always seems
that the lessons I work on the hardest
are the least interesting to my class.
I can see why many catechists
don't bother to plan very well.
Why should they?

Yet, I know deep down
that sharing my faith
and passing on the beliefs
and traditions of our church
is one of the most important things
I might ever do,
and I want to take it seriously.

Help me to believe
that even if the children
seem less than enthusiastic
I have to keep on trying.
And I hate to admit it,
but maybe I just haven't
    gotten it right yet.

Guide me, please, as I begin
    planning
yet another lesson for yet
    another class.
I know what the manual says,
but what do you want me to do or say
to touch hearts, to deepen faith?
May I listen
for your holy guidance
today and always.
Amen.

*Catechesis is,
after all, a process
of taking on a way
of life and personal
conversion, not
the acquisition
of a body of
information.*

General Directory
for Catechesis in
Plain English, #157

May I listen to you this day,
Holy Spirit.

LOOKING AHEAD TO LENT

Lent begins in two weeks.

Inspire me, Holy Spirit,
Spirit of Jesus incarnate,
to walk the lenten journey well
and to be a model and good example
for the children I teach.

I know that you forgive me
for the times I have been
    impatient or unfair,
but I really want to do better,
to be more open to the needs
    of every child,
to welcome each and respond to each
as a unique individual,
a precious gift from God.

Teach me how to pray
more sincerely and more often.
Teach me how to fast,
especially from all that might
    give bad example.
Teach me how to share my time
and my attention more
    generously. Amen.

*Jesus made himself
a catechist of the
kingdom of God,
announcing a
joyful message.
And now Jesus
sends us, just as
he did his own
disciples, to teach
as he did and to
announce his reign.*

General Directory
for Catechesis in
Plain English, #163

Holy Spirit,
please
prepare my
heart for
Lent.

MY ROLE IS IMPORTANT

Jesus, my Savior and companion,
    I do believe
that my role as a catechist is important.
I do believe that it is a call from you.
You have entrusted
these unique young individuals
to my love and care.
Each has the potential
to make the world a better place.
Yet, I can't help expecting
thanks and praise for what I do.
I want parents to acknowledge
the key role I play in their
    child's life,
and I want the children to
    love and thank me.
But, of course, this hardly ever happens.

Help me not to look for rewards,
but to dedicate myself to serving you
and the needs of others
as you have called me to do.
Deepen my faith in your call.
When I experience difficulties
help me to remember that
my role is important indeed. Amen.

The catechist must address those to be catechized in their real-life situations, no matter how diverse, making the gospel genuine nourishment for their lives.

General Directory for Catechesis in Plain English, #169

Deepen my faith in you, dear Savior.

WAITING FOR REBIRTH

How appropriate, dear God,
that Lent comes in winter.
Nature is at rest, sleeping and silent,
waiting for rebirth.
Lent is about biding time,
a time for reinforcing
and re-invigorating my faith.
It is that time in the church year
for walking with Jesus toward death,
and through death to resurrection,
to a stronger and livelier faith.

That's what I want for myself,
great and good God,
and that is what I ask for my class.
Help us to make the journey
    through Lent
united in prayer, fasting, and
    almsgiving.
Help us to make our way with Jesus,
as we confront our weaknesses,
and rejoice in our strengths.
May we pass with him through death
to the new and glorious life of Easter.
Amen.

The Christian life is one that requires constant renewal, which is the role that catechesis plays.

General Directory for Catechesis in Plain English, #171

Be with me on this journey, dear God.

TEACHING YOUR LEAST ONES

Jesus, loving friend and Savior,
you have said so clearly in Scripture
that what I do for your "little ones"
I do for you.
I find this hard to remember
especially when a child
is disruptive or loud or rude
or even just too playful.

I forget that you are with me
when a child is too slow or too unwilling
to learn or remember what
    I am teaching.
It's so much easier to believe
that you are present in those children
who are quick, bright, and well groomed.
The "nice" little boys and girls
are so much easier to teach!

Forgive me, Jesus,
when I fail to see your presence
in the messy, less-than-perfect children.

*The various stages
in the journey
of faith must be
properly integrated
into an ongoing
catechetical
experience that
begins at faith's
inception and lasts
for a lifetime!*

General Directory
for Catechesis in
Plain English, #171

Forgive me when I show preferences
and give me the courage
to love and teach every child
as you want me to love and teach.

May I reach out
to your "least ones"
in every class I teach.
This is my lenten resolution.
I can only keep it
if you help and guide me.
Amen.

I need you with me,
my friend and Savior.

THE STRUGGLES OF FAITH

Lord, Jesus Christ, son of the living God,
where are you when I need you?
I'm sitting here staring down
    at my lesson plan
knowing in my heart that it is dull.
There's nothing here that I
    would want to learn
were I the intended audience,
nothing here that would touch my heart.
So what should I do?
I need you to guide me,
to fire me up, to give me a boost.

I do believe in you; you know I do,
but I don't feel very enthusiastic
about my faith just now.

I think I will put this plan
    aside for a day or so,
while I wait for you to inspire me.
Open my heart to your Holy Spirit
and I will try to listen; I really will.
Speak to me, please,
for the sake of your children.
Amen.

The task of the catechist as an educator in the faith differs from all other ministries, even when fully coordinated with them.

General Directory
for Catechesis in
Plain English, #219

———————

Please
inspire me,
Lord Jesus.

PRAYER OPENS MINDS

Thank you, Holy Spirit, for
    all you do for me.
That lesson plan, that dull, dull plan,
ended up being one of my best lessons.
When I went back to it, I
    could see right away
that it lacked something essential.
There was no time for personal prayer,
for the children to encounter you.

When that became my priority,
the whole lesson took wing.
The children responded so well.
They welcomed the opportunity
    to pray quietly
with hands and hearts outstretched,
reaching for you.

This time of prayer also
    opened their minds.
They had more questions than usual,
and more enthusiasm too.
I never would have thought it.
Thanks again. Amen.

Catechesis is a responsibility of the entire Christian community and should not be the work of catechists... alone. Indeed, the entire community by the way it lives and acts and thinks, is engaged in the catechetical process.

General Directory
for Catechesis in
Plain English, #220

Thank you
for guiding
me,
Holy Spirit.

YOU ARE MY EXAMPLE

Jesus, great teacher and guide,
I'm feeling sorry for myself today.
I want to offer my time,
my talent, and my energy
to proclaim the truth of your gospel
but right now it seems like
teaching religion is a thankless task.

I don't like it at all
when I am criticized by parents
who don't know me personally.
They blame me when their children
don't know the "facts" about their faith,
when they don't know
how to say their prayers
or how to behave at Mass.

I don't like it at all when my DRE
forgets to say thanks
when I go the extra mile with my class.

Yet, you are my example, Jesus,

The vocation to catechesis springs from baptism and is strengthened by confirmation. Hence, laypeople participate in the priestly, kingly, and prophetic ministry of Christ.

General Directory
for Catechesis in
Plain English, #230

You did not try to defend yourself;
you did not make excuses.
You did not expect thanks.
Your love overcame your need to do that.

Help me to love those I teach,
and to put their needs before my own.
You know I'm doing the best I can.
Teach me how to follow you.
Show me how to better share
    my faith. Amen.

Show me how to follow you,
great teacher.

ACCEPTING MY LIMITS

Sometimes,
loving and gracious God,
I can't meet everyone's
    expectations of me.
My family and friends make demands
and rightly so.
But my DRE and other parish leaders
also make demands,
and of course the children I teach
make the most demands of all—
especially on my time and patience.

Sometimes my burden is too heavy,
and I don't carry it well at all.
The hardest thing for me is
dealing with my own expectations.
As long as I think it is up to me
to change children for the better,
all by myself,
I am setting myself up
to be disappointed and frustrated.

*To be called
to catechetical
ministry, affirmed
by the Church for
it, and dedicated to
it, is a high calling!*

General Directory
for Catechesis in
Plain English, #231

Help me, please, to remember
the example of Jesus at these times.
He was able to accept
    people as they were
and still love them very much.

Help me to accept those I teach
as they are
and to accept
my own limitations as well.
Amen.

Help me with my burdens,
gracious God.

WHEN IT ALL GOES WRONG

Teach me how to follow you, Jesus,
teach me how to teach.
One thing I have learned very
    well as a catechist
is that I am always in need
    of your guidance.
Just when I think I've got it down,
when I have prepared the perfect lesson,
I meet unexpected "surprises."
The child who never says a word
talks and giggles all through class.
The one who always answers eagerly
doesn't have a clue what I am asking.
No one wants to lead the prayer service,
no one offers spontaneous prayers.
No one wants to sing
and the procession to the prayer table
seems to last forever.
And yet, when it is all over,
someone has learned an
    important lesson.
Me.
Next time, I'll ask your guidance
before I leap into my planning.
Yes, Jesus, I most certainly need you.
Please, teach me how to teach. Amen.

The absolute summit and center of catechetical formation lies in learning how to communicate the gospel message effectively. Jesus Christ is the center of this.

General Directory for Catechesis in Plain English, #235

Show me how to rely on you, Jesus.

YOUR WONDERFUL SURPRISES

Jesus, my redeemer and king,
I praise your holy name
and I thank you
for your wonderful surprises.
And indeed it is a surprise to me
that something as difficult
as being a catechist
can sometimes give me such joy.

Today was one of those days.

The children and I talked about
Easter and resurrection.
I tried to be very honest with them...
I said that I don't know how to explain
your death and resurrection.
I believe that you died on the cross,
and I believe that God raised you up
on the third day,
but I admitted that I didn't
    understand it.

The children responded so well to this.
"We don't always understand
        everything either,"
one of them said,
"So don't feel bad."

Then we all prayed together
that our faith in you would grow
in spite of our inability
to fully understand it.

Somehow we all knew
that you were there among us;
no explanation was necessary,
and none was given.
Amen.

*It is Christ whom
we communicate
to others and
catechists must be
able to animate
the journey to
Christ which those
in their care are
making.*

General Directory
for Catechesis in
Plain English, #235

Be with me, Jesus,
as I share my faith.

Risen Savior, Jesus Christ,
I praise and thank you
for the great gift of your resurrection.
When all seems hopeless and even lost,
when winter seems to overpower spring,
I am buoyed by the glory
    of your new life.
It gives me hope that I too
    will have new life,
not only in the hereafter, but now.

Now as I prepare for my
    final religion lesson,
now as I recall each of the
    children in my class,
now because of the many joys
the children have given me
and the disappointments, too,
that forced me to grow.
Now as I plan our closing prayer service,
I ask you again for the gift of new life.

May my faith be new,
   my hope be new,
my love be new.
May my prayers to you be said
with restored faith, hope, and love.

May each child in my class
experience these gifts in me
and know that they can
   have them too.
You hold out such good things
   for us,
and your resurrection
   seals the promise
that it will all come true.
Thank you, risen Savior, thank you.
Alleluia. Amen.

Catechists lead those being catechized to know Jesus Christ as the Son of God and to desire the union with Christ that the sacraments of initiation celebrate.

General Directory for Catechesis in Plain English, #235

May my faith, hope, and love keep growing.

I NEED BALANCE!

Holy Spirit, giver of wisdom
    and knowledge,
enlighten me this day that I may teach
what you want me to teach.
I want the children to know
    about their faith,
the facts, the details, the
    prayers, the creeds.
But I also want them to love their faith.

I want them to know you
and to feel your presence
    and guiding hand.
I want them to praise and rejoice
when we pray together in class,
not for my sake, but because they believe
you are there with us.
I need from you the gift of "balance"
—which I have in such short supply.
Balance involves both wisdom
    and knowledge.
I can offer information,
but I must be wise enough
to know when enough is enough.
Oh great Spirit of all that is good,
teach me to be balanced in every
    class I teach. Amen.

Catechists enter into deep communion with the Church through their formation and faithfully pass on the faith while adapting it to cultures, ages, and situations.

General Directory for Catechesis in Plain English, #236

Teach me balance, great giver of wisdom.

THE END IS IN SIGHT

O God of loveliness, O God
    of heaven above,
how great your care for us,
    how great your love.

The end is in sight now, only
    a few more classes.
I'm glad, of course, to have
    reached this point,
but I'm also a little sad.
There is still so much I want to share…
about you, about faith, about the church,
about the liturgy, about prayer,
about the sacraments, about the saints,
about Mary, about the liturgical year—
there's just not enough time.

Help me to do what I can, holy God,
and may I use these coming weeks well.
Then, I hope and pray, when
    classes are over
the faith of these children
    will keep on growing,
because it is you who enables their growth.
Guide me and stay with me,
for you know so well what happens
when I do things on my own. Amen.

Catechists must work in the present moment in history with its values, challenges, and disappointments. Therefore they must have deep faith, an abiding love for the Church, and a great social sensibility.

General Directory for Catechesis in Plain English, #237

Guide me and be with me, O God of all good.

STILL LEARNING

Holy Spirit, giver of humility,
I want to look into each child's heart—
as if each were my own beloved child.
For my last two classes, I have
    arranged for an aide
to work with the children,
while I take each one aside
    for an "interview."
I want them to know that
    I care about them
and what they have learned.
I want to ask what they think
    about you,
about prayer and Scripture,
about the church and its worship.
I want to know if they
have learned anything at all.

Come with me, please,
that I might really listen.
It's one thing to ask,
quite another to hear the answers.
Be with me and so in me,
that each child feels your love
burning right through my eyes and heart.
Help me to listen; help me to learn
even as my classes come to
    an end. Amen.

Catechesis is not merely a matter of teaching but also of witnessing to faith and leading learners to life in Christ.

General Directory
for Catechesis in
Plain English, #237

Help me
to listen
and learn,
Holy Spirit.

AS THEY GO FORTH

O God of great surprises,
I made it through after all,
but not without your help, of course.

Bless each child as he or she goes forth
to new discoveries, new growth,
and new and deeper faith
    in you (I hope).
Watch over these children
and keep your hand on them.
Who knows what they might
    do if you let go!
Give them the joy of faith in you,
the warmth of your love,
the hope of your eternal promises.
And let these gifts carry them into life
ready for whatever challenges
    they must face.

Thank you for a year of growth for me.
I learned a lot, but I still have
    a long way to go.
Go forth with me, please,
I don't want to make the
    journey without you.
Amen.

*By having zeal
for the reign of
God, which Jesus
possessed, the
catechist grows and
matures constantly
in his or her
apostolic vocation.*

General Directory
for Catechesis in
Plain English, #239

Go forth
with me,
God of great
surprises.

The Breath of the Soul
Reflections on Prayer
JOAN CHITTISTER, OSB

This simple little book from a great spiritual giant is for every person who longs for authentic prayer to be the very breath of his or her soul.

144 pages, hardcover
$12.95 • order 957477

Blessed Are You
A Prayerbook for Catholics
GWEN COSTELLO

These unique and deeply moving prayers offer Catholics a way to tap into their rich prayer traditions while praying in contemporary terms.

136 pages • $11.95 • order 952605

Desires of the Heart
Prayers for Growing Faith
BILL HUEBSCH,
WITH LEISA ANSLINGER

These 48 prayer experiences helps readers develop their relationship with God and become aware of the many ways we encounter God in our daily lives.

145 pages, with music CD
$19.95 • order 955566

The Catholic Way to Pray
An ESSENTIAL Guide for Adults
KATHLEEN GLAVICH, SND

Here you will find all the inspiration you need to jump-start your prayer life as a Catholic. Highly recommended for all Catholic adults, and catechists in particular.

120 pages • $9.95 • order 957552

ORDER ONLINE AT
23RDPUBLICATIONS.COM